Virtual Apprentice

OCEANOGRAPHER

By Don Rauf
and Monique Vescia

Checkmark Books®
An imprint of Infobase Publishing

Virtual Apprentice: Oceanographer

Checkmark Books
An imprint of Infobase Publishing
132 West 31st Street
New York, NY 10001

The Library of Congress has cataloged the hardcover edition as follows:

Library of Congress Cataloging-in-Publication Data

Rauf, Don.
  Virtual apprentice. Oceanographer / Don Rauf and Monique Vescia.
     p. cm.
  Includes bibliographical references and index.
  ISBN-13: 978-0-8160-7895-0 (alk. paper)
  ISBN-10: 0-8160-7895-5 (alk. paper)
  1. Oceanography–Vocational guidance–Juvenile literature. I. Vescia, Monique. II. Title.
  GC30.5.R38 2007
  551.46023–dc22

                    2007019427

Produced by Bright Futures Press (http://www.brightfuturespress.com)
Series created by Diane Lindsey Reeves
Interior design by Tom Carling, carlingdesign.com
Cover design by Salvatore Luongo

Photo Credits: Table of Contents Kay Ransom; Page 5 Bucca Pino/Dreamstime.com; Page 7 Bettmann/CORBIS; Page 16 OAR/National Undersea Research Program; Page 19 Mountains in the Sea 2004, NOAA Office of Ocean Exploration, Dr. Les Watling, Chief Scientist, University of Maine; Page 22 Kay Ransom; Page 25 Gulf of Alaska 2004, NOAA Office of Ocean Exploration; Page 27 OAR/National Undersea Research Program (NURP); Page 30 Personnel of the NOAA Ship David Starr Jordan; Page 33 Tommy Schultz/Dreamstime.com; Page 36 Gulf of Alaska 2004, NOAA Office of Ocean Exploration; Page 40 Alexander Bahr.

Note to Readers: Please note that every effort was made to include accurate Web site addresses for kid-friendly resources listed throughout this book. However, Web site content and addresses change often and the author and publisher of this book cannot be held accountable for any inappropriate material that may appear on these Web sites. In the interest of keeping your on-line exploration safe and appropriate, we strongly suggest that all Internet searches be conducted under the supervision of a parent or other trusted adult.

Printed in the United States of America

VB BFP 10 9 8 7 6 5 4 3 2 1

This book printed on acid-free paper.

CONTENTS

The Wonderful World of Oceanography

People have always been curious about the ocean. Since prehistoric times, the ever-changing world of water that covers most of our planet has been a source of myths, legends, and folklore. The ocean has provided humans with a seemingly limitless food source, yet it creates hurricanes and tsunamis with enough force to wipe out entire coastal communities. Its mysterious powers inspire respect and fear, and even seafaring people familiar with the ways of the ocean have imagined fantastic monsters lurking in its depths.

Oceanography is the scientific study and exploration of the global ocean in all its aspects. This "young" science has developed fairly late in human history (compared to medicine or mathematics, for instance). In fact, more people have traveled into outer space than into the deep ocean. The most exciting discoveries in oceanography are yet to come.

Virtual Apprentice: Oceanographer immerses you in the most mysterious environment on Earth. Join the scientists who explore this vast and largely unexplored frontier, whether from the deck of a research vessel or a computer lab on dry land. Travel down into the deepest trench on the ocean floor and visit ghostly shipwrecks and weird "black smokers" towering above the seabed. Meet bizarre creatures that have adapted for life in different marine environments. Jump into the Virtual Apprentice experience for a day full of oceanographic challenges. Discover how some oceanographers are trying to protect the ocean's food supply while others are seeking alternative energy sources beneath the waves. Find out about the biggest challenges facing oceanographers in the coming decades, and learn what you can do to help preserve the oceans that sustain all life on Planet Earth.

Get set to plunge into the world of the oceanographer!

Is an underwater office in your future?

Diving Into Oceanography

Sonar was first developed in 1905 to help ships avoid icebergs, but interest in this listening device increased during World War I as a way to detect enemy submarines.

The first people to study the ocean— to make observations and record data—were, naturally enough, the ones who lived next to it, traveled across its surface, and gathered food from its waters. Over a period of roughly 25,000 years, the Polynesians navigated across thousands of miles of the Pacific Ocean as they colonized islands such as Fiji, Samoa, Tahiti, and eventually the Hawaiian Islands. How did they find their way across the open ocean without the help of compasses, chronometers, or any other tools of navigation? The Polynesians paid close attention to the directions of waves and currents, they noted the positions of the stars, and they knew which kinds of birds and animals lived in different parts of the ocean. With this information, they were able to make ocean maps, called *stick charts*, out of pieces of wood or bamboo. The stick charts used shells or knots to show the positions of islands.

In a different part of the world, seafaring peoples such as the ancient Phoenicians, and later, the Egyptians, the Romans, and the Greeks also gathered knowledge about the oceans. Much of Greece consists of islands, and many Greek myths and legends involve the ocean. The Greek philosopher

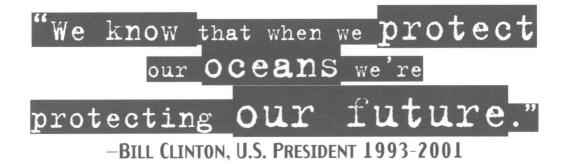

Aristotle (384–322 B.C.)—described the structure and habits of 180 species of marine animals. Some of his information is still considered valid today.

Many early ocean voyagers were trying to find and extend trade routes. Arabs navigated the Red Sea, the Persian Gulf, and the Indian Ocean in order to trade goods such as silk, pearls, spices, and slaves with people in Africa, India, Southeast Asia, and China. During the first part of the Roman Empire (which

Some early ocean explorers, like those in the Niña, Pinta, and Santa Maria, set out to discover new trading routes and lands.

began about 27 B.C.), merchant ships navigated trade routes with the help of a *periplus*, a chart listing ports and coastal landmarks with distances between.

In fifteenth-century China, an admiral named Zheng Ho explored much of the Indian Ocean, navigating with compasses and by the stars. Time on shipboard was measured by burning sticks of incense. During seven voyages between 1405 and 1433, his "Treasure Fleet" visited the great trading centers of India and Africa and helped China extend its control over much of Asia.

A School for Sailors

In 1416, Prince Henry of Portugal, known as Henry the Navigator, established Sagres, a center for the study of navigation and other oceanographic information, in southwestern Portugal. The explorers Christopher Columbus and Vasco de Gama were both students at Sagres. During Columbus's four voyages he collected and studied the marine animals and plants he and his crew encountered, and he noted currents and weather patterns.

During the period known as the Renaissance (meaning "rebirth") between 1492 and 1522, European explorers embarked on voyages that helped reveal the true extent of the earth. The Portuguese explorer Ferdinand Magellan made important contributions to oceanographic science when he sailed around, or circumnavigated, the globe between 1519 and 1522 and found that the Pacific Ocean was much larger than previously believed.

Most of these great voyages were undertaken for commercial reasons, paid for by governments and individuals eager to invest in the discovery of new sea routes for shipping goods between different countries. Commercial routes across the globe often followed the path of winds that sailing ships needed to push them around the planet. But not all of these voyages were fueled by profit alone. One navigator more interested in gathering scientific knowledge than in accumulating wealth was British captain James Cook (1728–1779). Between 1768 and 1779, Cook mapped much of the coastline of New Zealand, New Guinea, and the Pacific coast of Australia. He also charted many islands in the Pacific including the Hawaiian Islands, where Cook was killed by a group of native people following the death of a local chieftain, who had been shot by Cook's men.

Benjamin Franklin also contributed to the science of ocean-ography when, in the late 1700s, he was the first person to plot the course of the Gulf Stream. This so-called river in the ocean is a fast-moving current of warm surface water that sweeps north along the East Coast of the United States and then over the North Atlantic to Europe. Ships sailing from North America to Europe could almost double their speed by staying in this stream. Efforts to explore the polar regions and to find an elusive "Northwest Passage" through the frozen northern lands claimed many lives over the years. Finally, in 1903, Norwegian Roald Amundsen lo-cated a route that ships could safely pass through.

Reef Rescue

Here are 10 things you can do to help save a coral reef:

1 CONSERVE WATER. The less water you use, the less waste water that eventu-ally finds its way back to the oceans.

2 RECYCLE—anything and everything. If your community doesn't have a recycling program, start one. This will help reduce the amount of trash that ends up in the ocean.

3 DON'T POLLUTE. Never put garbage in the water, and don't leave trash on the beach.

4 HANDS OFF! If you go snorkeling on a reef, don't touch the coral. Hands and swim fins can damage delicate coral animals.

5 JOIN UP. Become a member of your local aquarium or zoo. Find out what they're doing to help save the world's reefs.

6 REPORT DUMPING or other illegal activities.

7 LEARN MORE about coral reefs. Find out how many species live in reefs, and how different medicines are found in reef organisms. Help others understand about the importance of reef preservation.

8 DON'T BUY RARE FISH. Only buy fish for your aquarium that have been collected in an ecologically responsible way.

9 SEND MONEY to support conservation groups working to save the world's coral reefs.

10 VOLUNTEER. If you live on the coast, volunteer for a reef monitoring program. If you live inland, help to save a river or a lake—all watersheds eventually affect the ocean and, in time, coral reefs.

The Birth of Modern Oceanography

The first modern oceanographer was U.S. Navy lieutenant Matthew Fontaine Maury (1806–1873). Sorting through a stockroom full of old ship's "logs," record books where navy captains dutifully recorded the speeds of their vessels and the directions of winds and currents, Maury realized that these records contained a wealth of information. By sifting through this data and noticing patterns, he was able to create ocean charts based on what he found He also devised a technique for determining the courses of various ocean currents: He asked sailors to put messages into bottles and note the ship's location when the bottles were tossed overboard. When the bottles washed ashore, the people who found them were directed to write Maury and tell him where the bottles were found. In 1855, Maury published the first textbook on oceanography, *The Physical Geography of the Sea*.

Meeting the Challenge

The Challenger expedition (1872–1876) was to oceanography what the Apollo missions were to space exploration. Two scientists, William Benjamin Carpenter and Sir Charles Wyville Thomson, convinced the British navy to supply ships for an ambitious scientific expedition. The ships were equipped with nets to collect animals at different levels and samplers to grab rocks and mud from the seafloor. Mechanical engines called winches (still essential equipment on research vessels today) were used to lower and hoist sounding lines to determine how deep different parts of the ocean were. During the four-year-long expedition, scientists learned more about the oceans than people had known

The Challenger expedition was to oceanography what the Apollo missions were to space exploration.

in all previous human history. This was the first oceanographic expedition to circumnavigate the globe, and the Challenger traveled to every ocean except the Arctic to take samples, record water temperatures, collect specimens, and make depth soundings. More that 4,400 new species of marine life were identified. The Challenger expedition discovered the deepest place in the ocean: a spot almost seven miles down in the western Pacific called the Mariana Trench (now called Challenger Deep in its honor).

Oceans Five

Five is a useful number in oceanography. The global ocean on Earth is divided on maps into five oceans (you can remember because there are five letters in the word *ocean*): The largest is the Pacific Ocean, followed by the Atlantic, the Indian, the Antarctic (or Southern), and the Arctic. People often use the words *ocean* and *sea* interchangeably to mean a large body of salt water. But a sea can be enclosed by land, whereas the global ocean covers the whole planet.

Oceanographers divide the ocean into five zones according to how far down sunlight penetrates:

1. The **epipelagic** or sunlit zone (0–660 feet): Plants can grow here.
2. The **mesopelagic** or twilight zone (660–3,300 feet): Some light penetrates; no plants grow.
3. The **bathypelagic** or midnight zone (3,300–13,200 feet): No light.
4. The **abyssal** zone (13,200–19,800 feet): Pitch-black bottom layer, almost freezing; immense pressure.
5. The **hadal** zone (over 19,800 feet): Water found in ocean's deepest trenches.

Most of the global ocean lies below the epipelagic or sunlit surface zone. Only a small fraction of the life of the ocean lives in or passes through this top layer.

Breathing Underwater

In ancient times, the oceans were used, as they are today, to move valuable cargo from one place to another. When a ship

CHECK IT OUT

The first organized efforts to study the world's oceans had to wait until 1736 and the development of an affordable chronometer, a spring-driven (rather than pendulum-powered) clock that keeps accurate time aboard ship, and allows the position of a vessel to be accurately pinpointed by latitude and longitude. That meant that if you were sailing in the middle of the ocean without any landmarks to guide you, you could still determine exactly where you were.

went down because of bad weather or enemy attack, all those goods went straight to the bottom of the sea. Some cargo might be recovered if a diver could stay down long enough to collect it and bring it to the surface. So people had to figure out a way that they could continue breathing underwater. Some solutions to this problem worked better than others.

Try this experiment at home, if you haven't already done it in one of your science classes. Hold an empty glass upside down over a container half full of water. Push the glass straight down; you'll see that, unless you tip the glass, the air stays in all the way to the bottom, keeping the inside dry. The diving bell works on the same principle, which ancient people understood. As far back as the fourth century, accounts describe the practice of using a barrel to trap air so that a person underwater would have a temporary air supply. Many years later, Edmund Halley gets the credit for inventing, in 1690, an early version of the modern diving bell. Halley's bell was large enough to accommodate several divers and could be resupplied with barrels of air from the surface.

In 1830, the "Standard" diving suit was invented, which is still used today. This weird-looking outfit features a heavy metal helmet with a round "porthole" for viewing. Oxygen is fed into the helmet from the surface through a long tube. The suit incorporates weights that keep the diver from floating to the surface. In the 1940s, SCUBA (which stands for Self-Contained Underwater Breathing Apparatus) was developed, which lets divers carry an air supply in tanks on their backs.

The farther you go beneath the surface, the greater the water pressure becomes. A scuba diver has to adjust the air pressure in her supply tanks in response to this pressure. If a diver surfaces too quickly, she can suffer from a painful and sometimes deadly condition called decompression sickness or "the bends." Despite the dangers of working underwater, scuba allows oceanographers to extend their underwater observations and to study different marine animals in their natural habitats.

The oceans have always been important in wartime. Armies and weapons can be transported by water, harbors can be blocked with ships, and supply lines cut off. Many tools and devices that oceanographers rely on were first developed for military use,

CHECK IT OUT

Scientific research vessels are sometimes named after characters in Greek legends. The submersible *Jason/Medea*, a ROV used to explore the deep ocean, is named after two figures in ancient Greek mythology: Jason, who sought the prized Golden Fleece on his ship, the Argo; and his wife, Medea. Captain Jacques Cousteau's ship, the *Calypso*, was named after a sea nymph in Homer's epic poem *The Odyssey*.

such as the submarine. Another, Sonar (short for Sound Navigation and Ranging), was used by the navy to detect enemy subs, but it became an essential tool for oceanographers, who used sound waves to determine how deep parts of the ocean were. This was a big improvement on the old system of depth sounding, which went like this: Lower a 200-pound weight into the water attached to miles of rope, wait until it hits bottom, measure the length of the line, then reel it in—a process that might take hours.

Deep-Sea Diving Devices

Submarines, which date back to the seventeenth century, were first developed for military use, as a means of avoiding detection and torpedoing warships on the surface. By World War I (1914–1918), nations such as Great Britain and France had large submarine forces that played a role in that conflict. In peacetime, some military subs have been adapted for oceanographic research. However, most research submarines are smaller and less powerful than navy subs and are outfitted for purely scientific purposes.

Certain oceanographers also make use of *submersibles*. Submersibles are different from submarines because they don't operate above the water, many are connected to a larger vessel by a tether, and they have a shorter range than subs. Otis Barton's "bathysphere" was basically a hollow steel sphere attached with a thick cable to a surface vessel. A rubber hose supplied electricity, air, and telephone wires to communicate with the surface. In 1934, Barton and William Beebe made a record-breaking descent in the bathysphere to a depth of 3,028 feet, where they saw "a world as strange as that of Mars."

The bathyscaphe is a self-propelled submersible invented in 1948 by the Swiss scientist Auguste Piccard. Twelve years later, in

Thanks for Smoking

People used to think the bottom of the sea was as barren as the surface of the moon. Then Robert Ballard discovered hydrothermal vents, fractures in the sea-floor that spew forth a hot soup of chemical compounds. These chemicals pile up into tall "chimneys" that scientists call *black smokers*. The undersea vents support unique ecosystems that run on chemicals (chemosynthesis) rather than on the sun's energies (photosynthesis). Conduct your own research and find out about three animals (scientists have identified more than 300 species) that live around hydrothermal vents. This interactive site is a good place to begin your research: http://www.divediscover.whoi.edu/vents/index.html.

1960, his son Jacques Piccard and Navy Lieutenant Don Walsh climbed into a bathyscaphe called the *Trieste* and descended, over the course of five hours, to Challenger Deep. The deep-diving record they set–35,810 feet–may never be broken.

Earth and Ocean in Motion

Most of the major discoveries of oceanography have occurred only in the last 50 years. Among these is the theory of plate tectonics, which helps explain how the earth evolves over time. The study of the deep ocean floor was key to the development of plate tectonics theory. It showed that seafloors are continually spreading, with new areas forming and older areas sinking back into the molten-hot core of the planet. Earth's surface is covered by a series of large "plates." These plates are continually moving in different directions and at different speeds and ramming into one another like (very slow-motion) bumper cars at an arcade. The places where the plates smash and rub together are the sites of earthquakes, volcanoes, mountain building, and the cause of ocean trenches. Because of plate tectonics, in 10 million years the cities of Los Angeles and San Francisco will be side by side!

In 1968, the goal of the first Deep Sea Drilling Project (DSDP) was to test the theory of plate tectonics. A special ship equipped with drills made cuts deep down into the seabed and removed long, skinny cores made up of layers of sediment. The subseafloor sediments in these core samples contained a rich and well-preserved record of the planet's past. Today, 30-foot-long core samples drilled from the seafloor are stored in the United States and Germany in "core libraries" for other scientists to study.

Oceanography Today

Oceanography is a complex science that casts a wide net, so to speak. It includes many different sciences: physics, chemistry, geology, zoology, biology, and others. And just as there are specialists in the fields of medicine and music and law, there are many types of oceanographers. If you worked in this field, you might specialize in one of these four "subfields," or areas of emphasis:

- **Biological oceanography** is the study of the multitude of creatures that live in the oceans (from single-celled microorganisms to blue whales, the largest animals on Earth) and their relationships to their ocean environment.

• **Chemical oceanography** studies the chemistry of the ocean and its chemical interaction with the atmosphere.

• **Marine geology and geophysics** is concerned with the study of the ocean floor, including plate tectonics.

• **Physical oceanography** focuses on the causes of various motions of ocean water such as currents, tides, and winds.

It is possible to work as an oceanographer and never set foot on the deck of a ship or don a wet suit and scuba gear to follow an octopus into an underwater cave. Plenty of oceanographers work on computers or in laboratories, and some of them don't even live near the ocean!

Big Fish

Unlike those of professional athletes or rap artists or politicians, most oceanographers' names are not known by the general public–with a few exceptions. Jacques Cousteau (1910–1997) started life as a sickly child with stomach problems and anemia. He hated school, but he loved to swim. By the time he died at age 87, this French oceanographer had done more than anyone else to raise people's awareness about the ocean and its wonders.

Cousteau once said, "The best way to observe a fish is to become a fish," and millions of viewers were able to follow his trail of bubbles down into some of the most amazing places on Earth. *The Undersea World of Jacques Cousteau* was an award-winning TV series that ran from 1966 to 1973. The show followed Captain Cousteau and the crew of the *Calypso* on their underwater explorations around the world.

Cousteau's legacy may be one reason why even kids who live in the Midwest, thousands of miles from any ocean, list "oceanographer" among their favorite professions. Oceanographers even refer to the "Cousteau syndrome"–the misperception that all marine scientists spend their days snorkeling around coral reefs.

FIND OUT MORE

Read the book that inspired Robert Ballard to become an oceanographer: French writer Jules Verne's sci-fi classic *20,000 Leagues Under the Sea*, first published in 1869. The book follows Captain Nemo as he explores the uncharted depths in his submarine *Nautilus*. Jacques Cousteau even called this book his "shipboard bible." Does Verne's story seem like pure fantasy to you or did he get some things right about the underwater world?

Dr. Sylvia Earle prepares to do underwater research in a submersible.

Sylvia Earle is an oceanographer who has "gone where no person has gone before" to explore the depths of the ocean. Known as the "Queen of the Deep," Earle has broken records for deep diving. In 1979, she made the world's deepest solo dive wearing an armored JIM diving suit especially constructed to withstand the tremendous pressure at those depths. Earle also spent weeks living with an all-woman team of "aquanauts" in the Tektite underwater laboratory on the seafloor of the U.S. Virgin Islands. She has written many books about her discoveries, some of which you might find in your school library. In 1998, *Time* magazine named Dr. Earle a "hero for the planet."

Some of the most exciting oceanographic adventures of the 20th century were lead by Robert D. Ballard, who calls himself a "high-tech, modern-day Captain Nemo." Like many future oceanographers, Ballard grew up on the coast, and he spent time as a child exploring the tide pools near his home in San Diego.

His most important scientific find was the discovery, in 1977, of hydrothermal vents, which have challenged scientists to reimagine the way that life on Earth began. But Ballard is best known for leading the team that discovered the wreck of the *Titanic* in 1985. Inside the *Alvin* submersible, Ballard and two crew members were able explore the broken remains of the giant vessel on the seafloor. With the help of *Jason Jr.*, a remotely operated vehicle (ROV) attached to a tether and equipped with a variety of cameras, they captured haunting images of the doomed ocean liner 74 years after it hit an iceberg and sank to the bottom of the North Atlantic. Four years later Ballard also located the *Bismarck*, a German battleship that was sunk by the British during World War II. The Jason Project, launched in 1989 by Ballard, uses technology to bring ongoing research expeditions right into the classroom so that students and teachers can experience in real time the discoveries that oceanographers and other scientists are making.

Oceanography and the Future of the Planet

Sylvia Earle says one of the great truths people were forced to confront in the twentieth century is that "the sea is not infinitely resilient." We have learned that the mighty ocean is far more fragile than we ever imagined. Even places people tend to think of as remote, "unspoiled" paradises have been devastated by pollution. The coral gardens of Kaneohe Bay on the island of Oahu, Hawaii, took thousands of years to form, but raw sewage dumped into the water managed to destroy this natural wonder in just a couple decades.

The global ocean is Earth's life-support system and essential to the health of the planet. Scientists agree that human beings, collectively, are having disastrous effects on the oceans. Oceanographers are helping us better understand the oceans and reduce the harmful effects of humans on marine environments.

If you've ever dreamed of doing something really heroic, why not become an oceanographer? It's a job that might actually help save the world.

CHAPTER 2

Oceanographer at Work

With the deck beneath your feet rocking violently and the spray of salt water stinging your eyes, it's a challenge to stick to the task in front of you. But somehow you keep pulling and pulling the net out of the ocean. As a biological oceanographer specializing in fisheries science, you're interested in the creatures of the sea and you're excited as you finally haul your net onto the deck. In the net wriggle pipefish, anchovies, mullet, and bluefish. You're studying how pollutants affect the fish in this area of the sea, so you're thrilled that you have captured such a range of creatures.

You're sailing aboard a small specially equipped research vessel in the waters off the coast of New England. For two weeks, it's been your home and work place. Most of the year you're working on land as a professor of oceanography, teaching, researching, and preparing for these expeditions. So now that you're at sea, you're loving every minute of it because you're spending night and day near your favorite subject: the ocean.

FUN FACTOID

"Tidal" waves are not actually caused by tides. Earthquakes and other disturbances occurring below or near the ocean floor trigger these massive waves.

Staying Shipshape

Research ships are a maze of hallways, stairs, and compartments. Food is prepared in the galley; you eat in a dining

—JACQUES COUSTEAU, OCEANOGRAPHER

room, sleep in a dorm room furnished with bunk beds, and relax in a lounge with a TV and DVDs. There's even a workout room. The ship comes equipped with a "wet" lab where you will take samples from the fish you catch. You work at large work tables and sinks in this well-lit space, which comes outfitted with racks for holding

Oceanographers often use sophisticated equipment like this IFE *Hercules* ROV.

Current Events

In May of 1990, the *Hansa Carrier* foundered in rough seas, and 21 cargo containers filled with new Nike sneakers plunged into the North Pacific. Six months after the cargo spill, shoes began showing up on beaches along the West Coast. Two years later, sneakers were found on shores of the island of Hawaii. Oceanographers determined that some shoes would eventually make it across the Pacific to Japan. Take a globe and pinpoint a location somewhere in the ocean where an imaginary cargo spill of soccer balls occurred. Look at the globe and try to guess on which coastlines those balls will wind up. Then consult a current map (you'll find one at http://www.onr.navy.mil/focus/ocean/motion/currents1.htm) to see if your prediction was correct.

sample containers and a refrigeration unit in which to store them. While you do the messy work in the wet lab, you do more mathematical and analytical study in the "dry" lab, a room dedicated to the computers and video monitoring equipment.

With a fresh load of fish on board, your fellow scientists and college graduate students get busy in the wet lab. Here your team busily cuts into the animals, extracting tissue samples. You must carefully label all samples with the date, location, time, and note which team member took the sample. You record similar information on a separate data sheet. You toil in close quarters with those on the ship, so a spirit of cooperation and collaboration is always necessary. As you cut samples and dissect fish, you chat with the other scientists about the weather. Weather weighs heavily on your minds when you're at sea. A violent storm can spell an early end to a research expedition. Plus, it can make even the healthiest sailors seasick.

You're especially concerned that the water doesn't get too choppy. It has been a little rainy lately, and tomorrow you want to deploy a sampling device into deep water. The device, called a Semipermeable Membrane Device (SPMD), collects contaminants such as polychlorinated biphenyls (PCBs), polyaromatic hydrocarbons, and organochlorine pesticides. The Environmental Protection Agency says billions of gallons of industrial wastewater is discharged into the ocean every day, and much of it contains these toxins. These can be harmful to marine sea life and to humans who eat fish and other seafood. You're going to put this SPMD device into the water for a week so it can measure the pollutants.

Later in the week, you plan on using a Remotely Operated Vehicle (ROV). Your ROV features a video camera and a still camera. A long cable, or tether, lets you lower the ROV to the seafloor and operate it, controlling its direction, speed, and depth. With this sophisticated gizmo, you record images of the ocean deep for later analysis.

Devices scientists use to measure and monitor the water are technologically advanced and very expensive. That's why you and your crew have received thorough training on how to operate them. You certainly do not want to break or lose this equipment. To deploy most of these devices, you must use heavy cranes and winches, which are aboard most research vessels. You also follow procedures to keep yourself and shipmates safe as you conduct your work and operate this equipment. Living and working on a ship demands that rules of conduct be followed to ensure the safety of all those aboard.

Land Ho!

Although life at sea offers thrilling moments, it's also very tiring, and after a couple weeks you're ready for a rest. You want to see more than just your boat and the ocean all around. As usual though, you'll start missing the open waters about a week after you're home. You know how lucky you are to have that experience. An associate of yours, a physical oceanographer studying how ocean currents affect climate, never leaves her office and has never been on the ocean. She uses computers and data to do her job.

On land, it's back to teaching classes and performing research. On the research end, you will examine the samples from the fish you caught. You plan to run a recently developed test that measures the accumulation of pharmaceutical and personal care products in fish and other aquatic organisms. Recently, other researchers used the test on fish living near the mouth of a river. They were alarmed at the amount of residue that they found in the fish from

Psychedelic Slugs

The nudibranch (pronounced nudi-brank, which means "naked gills") is one of the most colorful creatures in the ocean.

These slow-moving bottom dwellers scare off predators or camouflage themselves with a dizzying array of neon hues and fantastic patterns (check out the nudibranch gallery at http://www.sergeyphoto.com/underwater/nudibranchs.html). Some nudibranchs even give off aromas that smell like lemon, watermelon, vanilla, or flowers. More than 3,000 species of these wildly colorful sea slugs can be found worldwide. Do some research and see if you can determine the function of those funny fingers (called *cerata*) that some nudibranchs feature.

Oceanographers spend a lot of time on dry land analyzing data in the lab.

sleep aids, antihistamines, blood pressure medicine, and other drugs. Pharmaceuticals find their way to the ocean when unused amounts are disposed of by people and drug companies. Also, humans and animals who have taken drugs excrete compounds that their bodies don't use, and these can linger in the environment and find their way to ocean water. You and your graduate students will be looking in the marine animals you've sampled for damage to DNA, destruction of the liver, and changes in the reproductive organs. It's rewarding work because you know that your final research could help in the conservation of the planet. With solid proof that fish are becoming more poisonous and unfit for human consumption, you hope the government will be prompted to set limits on the pollutants that are dumped into our oceans.

The long and sometimes tedious process of testing and evaluating fish tissues and organs takes some endurance. But you must do it accurately and make detailed, careful records. You have to analyze many, many different samples to prove your points. Once you have accumulated a large amount of data, you can study your measurements using computers. You then interpret your findings and come up with a theory about what your research means. Finally, you'll write up your results in a scientific paper. Ultimately, you will want to get your research published in a scientific journal so other marine scientists will be read about it.

As a college professor, you also have teaching duties. You're teaching two classes this semester—one is an introduction to marine biology and the other is a more advanced course about pollution and sea life. For your classes, you prepare lectures and rely on strong oral communication skills to keep your students engaged. You also give tests and assign papers, which you must grade later. Most of your students are working on long thesis papers. You keep office hours once a week, so you can give them guidance on their research or answer questions they have about course material. You find it highly rewarding to teach students and empower them with a knowledge that can advance the field of oceanography.

The job involves administrative work as well. You have to attend meetings with other faculty to discuss classes being offered and campus affairs. You put together a budget each semester explaining your costs and predicting the amount you will need in the months to come. That's why you put a lot of time into grant applications. Grant funding pumps vital cash into your research programs.

In your spare time, you keep up with scientific publications and journals. You need to know about the latest advances in your field with regards to research techniques and new equipment. Later at night, when all your immediate tasks are done, you begin to look at plans for your next sea expedition many months from now. What route you take, the purpose of your study, the cost estimates, and other details all take time to figure out.

Now it's time to call it a day, satisfied that your work is making a difference in the world because the oceans are important to all the people and creatures that live on Earth.

CHAPTER 3

Oceanography Tech and Trends

This is a great time to be an oceanographer, as you can see from our sampling of some of the most exciting new technologies and trends in ocean science. Today, technological innovations are allowing oceanographers all over the world to work together to learn more about the global ocean and the challenges facing our changing planet. Just keep reading to see for yourself!

Alvin and the ROVs

When Robert Ballard explored the *Titanic*, he spent hours each day traveling down to where the broken ship rests in 12,000 feet of water: "I had to commute five hours a day to work, and I was only allowed to work for three hours before I had to go back up." It's not efficient to bring people down to those depths…and it's also potentially dangerous and very expensive. Manned submersibles such as *Alvin* can cost as much as $25,000 a day to operate. Today more oceanographers are using Remotely Operated Vehicles, or ROVs, to explore the ocean environment. A ROV tethered to a surface vessel can transmit information over an electrical or fiber-optic cable to scientists on board. These devices are equipped with lights,

FUN FACTOID

Research suggests that the supply of large fish in the seas has diminished by 90 percent since 1950.

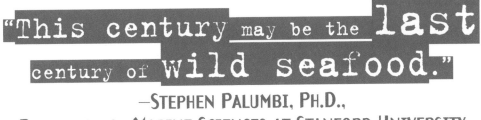

"This century may be the last century of wild seafood."

—Stephen Palumbi, Ph.D., Professor of Marine Sciences at Stanford University

cameras, various types of sensors, and mechanical hands that can grasp and manipulate objects. The ROV *Jason*, operated by the Woods Hole Oceanographic Institution, can work at a depth of 20,000 feet. The Japanese ROV *Kaiko* goes even deeper.

Submersible *Alvin* returning to the *Atlantis*.

Robotic Fleet

Sometime soon a fleet of 100 robotic submarines may be fanning out across the seafloor to study the 95 percent of this massive terrain that is still unexplored. A plan to ramp up study of the oceans by using autonomous underwater vehicles, or AUVs, was announced at a 2006 conference by NOAA, the National Oceanic and Atmospheric Administration. AUVs do not need to be tethered to another vehicle and can range over a great distance and require very little human supervision.

Satellite Tags

In order to protect endangered species of migratory animals, we need to know as much as possible about where they travel. Animals that range over huge distances or swim to great depths have been very tough to track, until now. A device called a satellite tag can be attached to a migrating animal such as a sea turtle, white shark, or whale. The battery-powered tag sends a signal to a satellite orbiting more than 620 miles above the surface of the earth, and the satellite relays data about the animal's whereabouts to scientists on land. Want to follow tagged animals on their journeys? Go to http://www.topp.org/topp-census.

Finding the Lost City

In 2000, an entirely new type of hydrothermal vent field, filled with ghostly white smokestacks, was located on the floor of the Atlantic Ocean. An oceanographic expedition returned to the "Lost City" in 2005, but most of the research team involved was thousands of miles away from the site. Remote technology allowed a team of ocean scientists at the University of Washington in Seattle to participate in

Working the controls of a remotely operated vehicle (ROV).

the exploration as it was happening via images transmitted from bottom of the ocean. (You can view images from this expedition at the NOAA Ocean Explorer Web site: http://www.oceanex plorer.noaa.gov/explorations/05lostcity/welcome.html)

Flip Out

It may look like a 355-foot-long baseball bat, but FLIP, which stands for Floating Instrument Platform, is actually a huge specialized buoy used by scientists at Scripps Institution of Oceanography. FLIP's unique design makes it much quieter than other research vessels and more stable in the water. Some of its missions have been to gather data about how storm waves are formed and to study sounds made by underwater animals. You can see how FLIP works at http://aquarium.ucsd.edu/Education/Learn ing_Resources/Voyager_for_Kids/flip/flip-gallery.

Virtual Dives

You don't need to live on the coast or be scuba certified to get a fish-eye view of the watery depths of the Monterey Canyon. You can sit in front of your computer screen and explore the marvels of the undersea world at http://www.mbayaq.org/efc/efc_mbari/mbari_resources.asp or surf the 'Net for other virtual dive sites.

Listen Up!

A U.S. Navy listening device called SOSUS, originally designed to detect Soviet submarines during the Cold War, is now helping to conserve the planet's oceans. SOSUS has been used to track the migrations of whales and to enforce the United Nations ban on drift nets, a fishing method that results in the unnecessary deaths of many marine animals.

As for recent trends, oceanography has moved center stage as the problem of global warming becomes increasingly urgent. As pack ice melts, rising sea levels pose a threat to coastal communities around the world. Many trends in ocean science today also concern the protection of ocean resources and marine biodiversity, the rich variety of organisms in the seas.

Sustainable Seafood

At the current rate of fishing, wild fish populations are in real danger of disappearing. If you eat a lot of seafood, make sure to choose fish and shellfish that aren't being overharvested. Download a seafood watch guide at http://www.mbayaq.org/cr/cr_seafoodwatch/download.asp. You can make sustainable choices when you're eating out, or give the guide to whoever does the food shopping at your house. In the words of marine biologist Stephen Palumbi: "Unless we fundamentally change the way we manage all the ocean species together as working ecosystems, then this century is the last century of wild seafood."

Life Under the Ice Sheets

When rising temperatures across the planet caused the collapse of the Larsen ice sheet in Antarctica, scientists got a glimpse of marine environments and sea critters that had been sealed off for many thousands of years. Among the exciting new species found

CHECK IT OUT

The Bay of Fundy in Nova Scotia boasts the highest tides on Earth, where the water can rise as much as 50 feet. See it for yourself! This Web site has a movie where you can watch the famous Fundy tide fall and rise as 1 billion tons of water move in and out of the bay twice a day: http://www.gma.org/undersea_landscapes/Bay_of_Fundy.

in these frigid waters were shrimp-like amphipods and a wildly colored octopus.

Free Willy

A growing number of people are speaking out against the practice of keeping *cetaceans*, marine mammals such as porpoises, beluga whales, and orcas, in tanks at marine parks. They argue that these animals, which typically range over large distances in the wild, are suffering in small tanks for the purpose of human entertainment. (While a dolphin may live up to 30 years in the wild, the average life span for one in captivity is only about four years.) More marine parks are rethinking this practice in response to public pressure.

Fish Farming

Over time, people evolved from hunters to farmers who raise land animals for food. Now we need to make the same transi-

---

What's Your Story?

You may have heard of a couple of famous oceanographers, such as Jacques Cousteau and Robert Ballard, but the names of most marine scientists are not household words. Their work may save the world, but the world may never know them. The job usually isn't about being in the spotlight. Does your personality suit this work? Look at the autobiography titles below and pick the one that best matches who you are:

1. *There's A Lot of Me in the Sea*
2. *The Fish Stickler: A Quiet Life of Underwater Study*
3. *Shallow Water: The Story of Me*
4. *Gill-Free Living: How I Quit Fish and Learned to Love Myself*

If you chose number 2, you're starting to think like an oceanographer! Remember: This job is *eco-friendly*, not *ego-friendly*.

tion in the sea, raising marine animals for human use rather than simply hunting them. As the numbers of wild fish continue to decline, ocean farming or *mariculture* will become an increasingly important means of feeding the world's growing population. Marine organisms now being farmed include seaweed, mussels and oysters, shrimp, salmon, and other species of fish.

Oceanographers with Horns

Recently, scientists have enlisted an unlikely ally in their efforts to learn more about the oceans: the narwhal (pronounced *narwall*). These strange marine mammals, known for the long, spiral tusk that male narwhals have, exist only in certain areas of the Arctic. Narwhals have proved difficult to study because of the remoteness of their habitat and because they dive so deep to feed: 5,400 feet down to the bottom of Baffin Bay in Greenland. By attaching scientific instruments to the narwhals, oceanographers are using the animals themselves to collect information about the ocean.

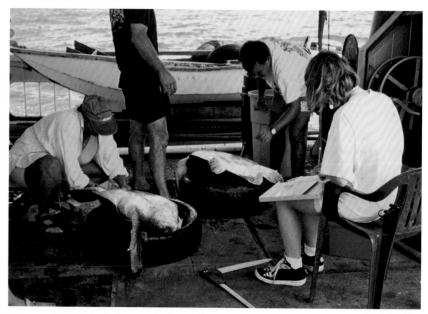

Researchers bring marine turtles aboard for genetic sampling and tagging.

Ocean Energy

The global ocean contains vast resources of energy in the form of waves, tides and currents, salt, and even temperature variations. This last source of energy has already been tapped using OTEC, or Ocean Thermal Energy Conversion, systems. An OTEC system uses the temperature differences in ocean water to (ultimately) generate electricity. Two useful byproducts of OTEC systems are nutrient-rich seawater that can support fish farming and cool water that can be used for air-conditioning.

A Cure for Cancer?

Nearly half the drugs in your family's medicine cabinet came originally from land plants. The oceans are very different chemically from land environments and may contain unknown substances that can be used to cure diseases and otherwise benefit human life. Drug companies have begun looking to the oceans for the next generation of pharmaceutical compounds. One chemical that might be used to treat breast cancer and some types of leukemia has been found in a Caribbean sea sponge.

Sea of Debris

When Captain Charles Moore sailed over some of the most remote parts of the Pacific Ocean, he expected to find only endless stretches of open water. What he discovered instead was floating plastic garbage, as far as the eye could see. The North Pacific subtropical gyre, a great spiraling current, has trapped drifting plastic debris and concentrated it into an area roughly the size of the state of Texas! Moore says, "I now believe plastic debris to be the most common surface feature of the world's oceans." Think about that the next time you go shopping, and avoid buying items packaged in non-recyclable plastic containers that might one day find their way into the ocean.

CHAPTER 4

Oceanographer in Training

Do you collect seashells at the seashore?

Maybe you love to bodysurf or ride the waves on a boogie board. Or do you spend hours with your nose pressed against the tanks at the aquarium, gazing at the colorful fish? If you feel mysteriously drawn to the sea, and you possess a curious mind and an interest in science, the ocean may be calling you with an exciting career opportunity.

Although people have explored the oceans since early times, these vast waters still hold many mysteries that oceanographers are trying to solve. To this day, scientists cannot explain monster rogue waves or where baby sea turtles go during the first few years of their lives. For centuries, sailors have witnessed times when the ocean glows intensely in all directions. Researchers still cannot explain this phenomenon. A career in oceanography can be a great adventure because you may uncover nature's best-kept secrets.

Getting Your Feet Wet

Even if you're a young student, you can dip a toe into the career waters early on. Because the job is all about water, it's a good idea to be a strong swimmer. Scientists often want to

FUN FACTOID

A mouthful of seawater may contain millions of bacterial cells, hundreds of thousands of phytoplankton, and tens of thousands of zooplankton.

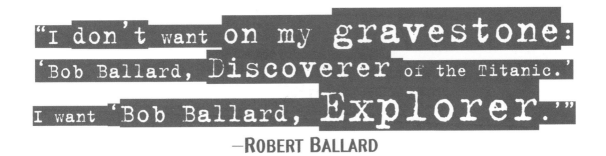

"I don't want on my gravestone:
'Bob Ballard, Discoverer of the Titanic.'
I want 'Bob Ballard, Explorer.'"
—ROBERT BALLARD

study life below the surface of the water, so you may want to gain experience swimming with flippers, a mask, and a snorkel. Researchers use snorkels in tropical waters to view colorful fish and coral. Sometimes oceanographers dive deeper to explore sea environments. In these cases, they wear scuba gear. If you're serious about ocean exploration, private training centers around the country offer lessons in scuba diving to kids starting at about age

Scuba-diving skills are a must for aspiring oceanographers.

10. Also, if you have a chance to sail on a boat, take it. Researchers often go out to sea for weeks at a time, so it's good to build your sea legs and know your way around a vessel.

Want to learn about marine life up close? Aquariums run educational programs for young people where you get to touch aquatic creatures such as live starfish, stingrays, and eels. There are even junior sea camps where you can snorkel and start to identify hundreds of fish, from the kelp bass to the blue-banded goby. Educational programs usually have you examine samples under microscopes, too. You learn that the plant life is just as important as the animal life in the survival of our oceans. Algae or seaweed, in fact, is one of the most important parts of the ocean's ecosystem. Any real-life experience gained in classes at aquariums and sea camps can help prepare you for a future in oceanography.

Even if you're not near the ocean or an aquarium, you can read up on sea science in books and magazines like *National Geographic*, *Oceanography* magazine, and *Discover*. You can rent documentaries on underwater exploration, too.

Set Your Coursework

Careers in oceanography are generally for students who rise above C-level. You have to hit the books and earn A's and B's. In junior high and high school, focus on your science and math classes. Take chemistry, earth science, biology, physics, and computer science. During labs for biology and chem classes, you'll analyze samples with microscopes, test tubes, and other scientific equipment, which provides perfect prep for real-world laboratory research. Don't skip English, either. An oceanography career can sink on bad communication skills. Those who know how to write persuasive papers and make powerful oral presentations rise to the top.

Go Wild!

To explore nature, scientists have to leave their labs and get out into the wild where they collect samples and take a close look at creatures and plants. Preparing for these expeditions takes some planning. Try plotting your own adventure. It can be a hike with friends to a local park or a night camping out in your backyard. Make a list of what supplies you'll need: food (popcorn, donuts, gummi sharks), gizmos (flashlight, cell phone, Game Boy), entertainment (comic books, harmonica, water balloons). Add a little science exploration if you can—find the most different kinds of leaves or stones, or observe insects in the grass and under logs. If you can handle a mini-trek, you'll have some idea what it might take to get ready for a big scientific trip.

If your school has a science fair, sign up and take the challenge. Science fair projects introduce you to basic scientific inquiry and research approaches. In a science project, you're doing tests to find an answer to a question. You're observing and recording observations and forming hypotheses which, of course, is excellent preparation for a scientific career.

If you're serious about studying the ocean in high school, here are a few specific programs you should look into:

Coastal and Ocean Science Training Internship Program (COAST). COAST is a summer learning experience that teaches about the coastal environment. The program provides an opportunity to challenge yourself and try new activities while getting hands-on experience working in one of North America's most pristine and diverse habitats. For more information go online to http://www.nosb.org/?anchor=coast.

National Ocean Science Bowl (NOSB). Teams from more than 350 schools across the United States compete for prizes, scholarships, and internships by answering ocean-related questions in this challenging competition. Go online to http://www.nosb.org to find out more.

Naval Science Awards Program. NSAP is a U.S. Navy and Marine Corps program that encourages students to develop and retain an interest in science and engineering. The program awards prizes and scholarships each year to selected high school students who exhibit their projects at science and engineering fairs. For more information go online to https://onronline.onr.navy.mil/pls/nsa/nsa.nsa.

The Hutton Junior Fisheries Biology Program. Sponsored by the American Fisheries Society, this program offers mentoring to high school students who have an interest in fisheries science. Students selected for the program are matched with a professional mentor in their area for a summer-long experience in a marine or freshwater setting. For more information go online to http://www.biosci.ohio-state.edu/~ocafs/OCAFShutton.htm.

FUN FACTOID

Anything living in the deepest part of the ocean—36,000 feet below sea level—must survive eight tons of pressure pushing down on every part of its body. That's the equivalent of one person trying to support 50 jumbo jets.

Marine biology students working on a homework assignment.

Additionally, the Marine Biology Web lists a number of region-specific intern programs available to students interested in marine biology. For more information go online to http://life .bio.sunysb.edu/marinebio/mbweb.html.

Deeper Learning Through Higher Education

Oceanography requires a four-year college degree. Most scientists have at least an undergraduate degree with a major in oceanography, biology, physics, chemistry, geoscience, mathematics, or engineering. Your college courses should emphasize mathematics, chemistry, physics, biology, geology, environmental dynamics, and possibly naval engineering. Nothing beats direct experience, so when it comes time to apply to college, look into what real-world research you can get involved with. In a college internship, you could spend weeks tagging turtles, tracking dolphins, or measuring pollutants. Also, join professional associations because they give you a chance to meet real scientists working in the field.

In college, you'll learn about the oceans in great depth—the chemical nature of sea water; the causes and effects of currents, tides, and waves; animal and plant life in the sea; and features of the ocean floor. Conservation is a hot topic—scientists want to help protect fish and other sea creatures that are endangered.

A lot of your coursework will depend on what you specialize in—biological, chemical, physical, or geological oceanography. Your degree will depend on what you study. You can be an oceanographer with a degree in marine geology, marine biology, physics, or environmental science, for example.

College students spend plenty of time collecting samples and then analyzing them in labs. Research often relies on sophisticated new equipment. An acoustic Doppler current profiler measures the velocity of currents, and a gravity corer measures properties of ocean sediment. Computers are used all the time in research, for analysis, and 3-D modeling. Research projects also give a chance to work in teams, and teamwork and collaboration is very important when in comes to studying the ocean. Students also learn about ship procedures and navigation. In a program called SEA Semester, at Woods Hole Oceanographic Institution (WHOI), students sail on wind-powered ships to the deep ocean to learn about the sea and conduct research projects. As you continue with your education, your studies advance. You may examine the relations between humans and marine life, energy resources in the oceans, and maps of the ocean floor.

Oceanographers often go beyond four-year college and earn graduate degrees. In the United States, the three top oceanographic research institutions are Scripps Institution of Oceanography (SIO) in San Diego, California, Woods Hole (WHOI) in Massachusetts, and the School of Oceanography at the University of Washington in Seattle. You might attend one of these schools and become a doctor of oceanography and marine biology.

Navigating your way to a higher education is no easy task. The American Meteorological Society offers a great list of colleges and universities at http://www.ametsoc.org/amsucar_cur ricula/index.cfm. Another educational route for oceanographers is through the Navy. Investigate opportunities at their Web site (https://www.onr.navy.mil/careers).

CHAPTER 5

Other Fish in the Sea

Oceanographers may be the authorities on the world's biggest bodies of water, but they are not the only experts in the sea. There are scores of other careers involving the ocean and its underwater inhabitants. In fact, most oceanographers rely on other professionals to collaborate with and complete their research. If you love the ocean but think oceanography may not be for you, investigate these related occupations:

Aquarium Director

Aquariums are basically zoos for fish and other creatures that live in and around the ocean. Directors serve as the "zookeepers" who oversee the aquariums. They are in charge of all the workers and decide what creatures will be on display in the tanks. They frequently come from teaching backgrounds, but they also need to be business-minded, thinking of new exhibits and ways to attract paying customers. Often, aquariums have a department devoted to ocean research. The Monterey Bay Aquarium has a research institute that studies marine life and other features of the ocean off the California coast. To find out more about this career, visit the Web site for the Association of Zoos and Aquariums at http://www.aza.org.

FUN FACTOID

The relative thickness of the hydrosphere, the layer of water and water vapor in the atmosphere that surrounds the earth, is equivalent to that of a coat of paint on a bowling ball.

"Underwater, every spoonful of water is filled with life."

—SYLVIA EARLE, OCEANOGRAPHER

Archaeologist

These scientists comb the globe in search of artifacts from past civilizations and cultures. Sometimes, their search for relics takes them beneath the waves and along coastlines. Portions of the Royal Quarter of Alexandria, for example, rest beneath the Mediterranean off the coast of Egypt. To study the ruins and statues of ancient Alexandria, archaeologists put on scuba gear and explore beneath the sea. Underwater archaeologists should be expert divers. Most have earned college degrees in archaeology and have a passion for historical research.

Commercial Diver

For the real adventure seekers, diving under the ocean offers many thrills. Commercial divers have mastered the use of scuba gear to breathe underwater. Deep-sea divers assist oceanographers with research, collecting samples, surveying, and testing the water. Some learn underwater welding so they can help build structures at sea, such as the drilling platforms used by oil companies. You can earn basic scuba-diving certification in about two months' time; even young adults between the ages of 10 and 14 can get Junior Open Water Diver Certification.

Computer Engineer

More and more, oceanographers rely on computers to study the ocean. Although some scientists have advanced computer skills, many turn to trained computer engineers to assist with their studies. Research requires accumulating lots of data, and computers help in analyzing this information. Computer experts can take information about the ocean waves and create computer models of

NAME: Stacy DeRuiter

OFFICIAL TITLE: Teaching Assistant

What Do You Do?

I'm a teaching assistant and a graduate student working in a joint program between the Woods Hole Oceanographic Institution (WHOI) and Massachusetts Institute of Technology (MIT). I help teach biological oceanography for first-year students. I just love working with students and getting to know the material in order to present it.

When I'm not teaching, I'm working on my research. One of my biggest projects is to design a tag for harbor porpoises. They are the littlest of all the dolphins and porpoises that live around here. I'm trying to build an electronic tag that records acoustic data—all the sounds the porpoise hears and makes. The tag also will record position data—how the animal is tilting and turning and how deep the animal is. I am working with help from an electrical engineer to create the tag—I could never do this on my own.

Most of my research has to do with how porpoises use *echolocation* for foraging rather than how they communicate. Echolocation is when the animal makes a sound and waits for echoes to bounce back. They hear an echo and can tell what direction it came from. Based on its properties, they can tell if it's a jellyfish, squid, or whatever. Basically, they see using sound. My porpoises are living in shallow water so there's lots of clutter—nets, rocks, seaweed— that affect their echolocation.

How Did You Get Started?

I didn't grow up wanting to be a marine biologist, but I wanted to do something with biology and exploring the natural world. I grew up in Grand Rapids, Michigan, near the Great Lakes. I wasn't near the ocean, but I always did have a fascination for large bodies of water. I did well in science classes, and I majored in biology and environmental studies in college. I did an internship studying the genetics of an Antarctic fish, and I got accepted into the program at WHOI. This is exactly the kind of field I want to work in—something where I can investigate interesting biological problems and connect them to environmental aspects.

them. Scientists then use these models for wave forecasting—they predict the height of waves, their frequency, and their strength. Programmers and software engineers have also developed interactive, 3-D simulations of the ocean that help students train in physical oceanography.

Environmental Ecologist

If you like science and have a commitment to saving the planet, this may be the career for you. An ecologist can study how pollutants and temperature change the ocean and the organisms that live there. They collect and study samples. If they detect pollutants in their samples, ecologists make recommendations on how to improve water quality. Sometimes, environmental ecologists work as ecological modelers as well. Modelers rely on mathematical modeling, systems analysis, and computer techniques to study the environment.

Fish Farmer

These experts work in the field of *aquaculture*, breeding, raising, and selling fish as a "cash crop." Because fish are their livestock, farmers are concerned with reproduction, feeding, disease management, and economics. Those who raise fish in the sea treat the salt water like their soil, paying close attention to what nutrients and conditions make for healthy waters. Their products range from shellfish grown in natural sea beds to salmon housed in large indoor tanks. Fish farmers must follow legal guidelines for raising fish, and they have to know how to deal with farm dangers such as excessive nutrients and natural predators. They also need a head for business as they sell their goods to the public in markets and restaurants.

Hydrologist

Hydrology means the study of water. Scientists in this field understand all about the movement, distribution, and quality of water. They may focus on how water evaporates from the ocean, forms clouds, and travels to other parts of the earth. Or their specialty may be acid rain. Acid rain droplets contain pollutants, which can cause an overgrowth of plant life where rivers enter oceans, drastically altering the natural environment.

Instrumentation Technician

These professionals help the engineers who design oceanographic equipment. They may test and assemble submersible chemical analyzers (devices that detect nutrients in the water) or underwater vehicles. Technicians tend to be mechanically inclined, and while some college engineering courses provide proper training, techs do not need a college degree to enter this field.

Marine Technician

Marine technicians are the auto mechanics of the boating world. They specialize in repairing small engines that power motorboats. This is very hands-on work, and you can often get trained in a two-year program after leaving high school. Most ships run on diesel power, so marine techs often specialize in diesel engines and marine propulsion technology.

Maritime Lawyer

Some waters are international and can be traveled by all boats. Other waters belong to specific countries and ships cannot pass through them without permission. These rules are all part of ocean or maritime law. Ocean law and policy includes seabed issues, navigation, shipping, maritime boundary issues, and marine scientific research. Law requires strong analytic ability, attention to detail, and an interest in negotiations, arguments, and justice. Those who focus on ocean law also have a fascination with the sea, and they must be committed to pursuing an advanced degree.

Meteorologist

If you love spending a Friday night glued to the Weather Channel, then meteorology may be for you. These scientists study the atmosphere and weather. Some concentrate on how the oceans change the

Pick Up the Pieces

FIND OUT MORE

Each year 160,000 volunteers from 33 countries participate in the International Coastal Cleanup. The first all-volunteer beach cleanup in the United States took place in Oregon in 1984. A lot of beaches and waterways rely on volunteer workers to stay garbage-free. Some organized cleanups are part of a monitoring system that records the types of trash that appear on the beach and tries to determine where it's coming from. Volunteer for a beach (or river, or creek) cleanup in your area. These events can be a lot of fun, and you will be amazed by the stuff that people throw away that winds up fouling beaches or clogging waterways.

NAME: **Bill Taylor**

OFFICIAL TITLE: **Fish Farmer**

What Do You Do?

I'm the owner of Taylor Shellfish (the largest shell-fish farming company on the West Coast). We have about 500 employees with operations in Puget Sound, Canada, Mexico, Hawaii, Fiji, and Hong Kong. The biggest single item we harvest is steamer clams or manila clams. We harvest a lot of oysters, mussels, and geoduck (a large clam—pronounced "gooey duck"). Most harvesting is done by hand. We use some machinery but really very little.

You have to make sure you're putting out a good-quality product and that your labor is being done efficiently. You always have to watch your crops to make sure they're growing well and make sure that they're not being eaten by predators, such as crabs and starfish. We have to monitor for red tide and pollution problems as well. We test for them all the time to make sure our food is safe to eat.

Mine isn't a normal day. Lots of times I'm jumping on an airplane to go to one of our locations, or I might be going to Washington, D.C., to lobby about permits for our farming activities. We also have to deal with regulations for how we handle shellfish processing and water quality. We've been working on a settlement with the Puget Sound Indian tribes over the rights to the shellfish. It's been fun working on growing geoduck and mussels that no one has grown before.

How Did You Get Started?

My great-grandfather started the business in the 1890s. I'm the fourth generation that has been involved with it. The business has grown, but in many ways it hasn't changed in 100 years. I enjoyed working with shellfish since I was a kid. I got serious about it at the end of my high school years. Shellfish farming is fairly unique, and it's one of the best sources of protein and good minerals. Shellfish feeds on algae in the water—so it's really good food. It feeds on such a low place on the food chain and you end up with such a good protein product. I think it's going to be an exciting area as more and more people start to live on the earth and they need to find new ways to get food for everyone.

ON THE JOB

NAME: Sid Macken

OFFICIAL TITLE: Underwater Videographer

What Do You Do?

I do freelance underwater videotaping. I do some of my own productions on historical topics in diving. I'm getting ready to start on one this summer. It will be an underwater tour of the state of Oregon from the lakes to the ocean. I've done work for public broadcasting in Portland. I taped the Oregon Department of Transportation bridge inspection team. Every year they go around inspecting the underwater footings of bridges. My job combines diving, editing, and videotaping. I do all my editing on computer now. I use a Sony DV camcorder in a special waterproof housing.

Any time I'm in the water I'm shooting pictures. I can find something interesting to look at wherever I dive. Octopus is my favorite animal that I've filmed. Some of the biggest octopuses in the world live in the Pacific Northwest. They're intelligent and curious. They really interact with you.

ON THE JOB

How Did You Get Started?

I got interested in diving when I was 10. I grew up in a farming community far from the ocean in rural Oregon, but for some reason the diving bug bit me. I started poking around in farm ponds and creeks and reading everything I could on it. I took scuba lessons when I was 13. I was fortunate to find an instructor locally. My first open water dive was a disaster. We went to a little cove on the Oregon coast. I was 14. I lost my swim fins out in the ocean. When I was in high school, I picked up my first amphibious 35mm camera. I've worked outside the diving industry for a long time as machinist and a 911 dispatcher, but I always stuck with underwater photography. I also got involved on the dive teams for two local sheriff's departments and a fire department. I went through dive rescue specialist training. I became an instructor to teach public safety diving. I did a lot of searches for people who drowned, for cars that had fallen off ferries or had been stolen, and for evidence from crime scenes. Once I dove searching for part of a frying pan that was used as a murder weapon. A fellow diver found it. Now, I'm doing what I really like—photographing underwater.

weather and how the weather can affect the oceans. Changes in ocean temperature can alter weather patterns around the world. El Niño is a major warming of the Pacific Ocean near the equator. When these waters heat up, more rainfall comes down. In the past, El Niño has produced dangerous hurricanes. Meteorologists and oceanographers work together to study ocean and atmosphere to better predict these hurricanes and other harmful conditions.

Ocean Engineer

Buoys, ocean seismometers (instruments that measure seafloor movement), underwater video equipment, acoustic measuring devices, stationary platforms for drilling and mining, and underwater vessels. These are some of the devices, vehicles, and structures that scientists rely on to explore the sea. But they would not be possible without the design skills and technological smarts of the ocean engineers who build them. Those who follow an engineering career path generally have a knack for numbers and math and enjoy building things with their hands.

Petroleum Engineer

More than 30 percent of American oil comes from offshore drilling. Oil companies hire petroleum engineers to help mine offshore oil and gas reserves. They take samples from the ocean floor to determine where oil and gas reservoirs may be trapped. Relying on their knowledge of the ocean, engineers figure out the best approaches for constructing oil wells at sea.

Seismologist

In their research projects, oceanographers can work with many different types of scientists. Some work with seismologists who

Don't Rock the Boat

Did you know that the word *nautical* and the word *nausea* come from the same ancient Greek word *naus*, which means *ship*? For thousands of years, the motion of the ocean has made some people ill. As an oceanographer, though, you may have to do some work at sea. Do you have the stomach for it? Ask yourself: Have you ever felt like you'd lose your lunch in a rowboat at the park or a canoe at camp? Do you even turn a little green in a wading pool, or on the school bus? (Some say that seasickness is closest to carsickness.) Then research at sea may not be for you. But don't despair—there are plenty of landlubber jobs in the marine sciences.

are earthquake experts. Earthquakes under the ocean can cause deadly and devastating tsunamis. On December 26, 2004, a giant undersea earthquake unleashed a series of tsunamis in the Indian Ocean, which killed more than 275,000 people. Working together, seismologists and oceanographers hope to better predict underwater earthquakes and understand how they work.

Ship's Captain

Sometimes called the skipper or master, the captain commands a ship. He or she is the decision-maker who gives orders to the crew and determines direction and speed at which a vessel will travel. In oceanography, the captain guides the vessels on which scientists sail. But captains also control ships carrying cargo, fishing vessels, cruise ships, tugboats, and more. They have a complete mastery of how ships operate and the laws of the sea.

Underwater Acousticians

In this highly specialized career, experts use sound to detect the location of fish, to map the seafloor in order to pinpoint the safest passageways for supertankers, to explore the earth's geological formations, and to search for oil deposits beneath the ocean floor.

Underwater Photographer

The Undersea World of Jacques Cousteau was the first program of its kind to show the possibilities of underwater photography. Underwater photographers and videographers combine a mastery of photography with underwater diving and exploration. They depend on special cameras and camera casings that are waterproof and pressure proof—especially for deep-sea photography. They must also be expert divers, and they typically have some scientific knowledge of the ocean and its creatures because they often take photos for science-related publications and programs.

CHECK IT OUT

Legends tell of the lost city of Atlantis, an ancient and advanced island civilization that suddenly disappeared beneath the waves. While many dismiss these tales as fiction, some people aren't so sure. Modern expeditions have attempted to search for the remains of Atlantis, pointing as evidence to the odd flight patterns of migrating birds that seem to circle a landmass that isn't there.

NAME: Usha Varanasi

OFFICIAL TITLE: Director of Northwest Fisheries Science Center, part of the National Marine Fisheries Service

What Do You Do?

I conduct and lead research to support the management and conservation of the Pacific Northwest's fishery resources. I oversee the science center and about 400-plus scientists, as well as five research stations. I am really a science enabler now rather than a doer. I'm helping others with research and chemistry analysis. We analyze salmon population trends. We are involved in the aftermath of oil spills. I started as a junior scientist working on oil spills, in fact. Because I came from a chemistry background I was looking at fish tissues after they pass through an oil spill. I was interested in what happens to those chemicals in the fish.

How Did You Get Started?

I grew up in India. I had a woman principal who said that girls should do whatever they are interested in because they can do as well as any boys. I was very good in chemistry and I liked mathematics. I always liked science because it's like a mystery story. You have pieces of the puzzle and you investigate it. I went to the United States to study, and I finished my degree in chemistry at the University of Washington. When I looked for a job in chemistry, there weren't many opportunities. However, there was an opening for a chemist to research the chemical composition of the fat in the heads of marine mammals, such as porpoises and whales. Their heads are filled with a very fatty tissue. Scientists were trying to see if the fatty tissue plays a role in echolocation. Fish wasn't exactly my field. I had never even heard the word *porpoise*. When I interviewed for the job, I was thinking "porcupine." I went home, looked up porpoises, and thought, OK, I would try this job out. [At work] I was surrounded by all these fisheries scientists, and I was always learning from them. I started to learn that if something is there, it is there for a reason. The fatty tissue, as it turns out, helps porpoises and whales with echolocation. I love scientific inquiry: Why is something happening, how is it happening? It's all very exciting.

ON THE JOB

CHAPTER 6

Kids Ask, Oceanographers Answer

To find out what our readers really want to know about a career in oceanography, we went to the source and asked actual kids what they would ask the experts. A group of home-schooled kids from Asheville, North Carolina, far from the waves and beaches, furnished us with questions, which we passed on to two experienced oceanographers—Dr. Rick Keil and Dr. Stace Beaulieu.

Dr. Rick Keil is the associate director of the School of Oceanography at the University of Washington in Seattle. He is a chemical oceanographer and the head of the Keil Lab and focuses on microbes in aquatic environments.

Dr. Stace Beaulieu is a research specialist in the biology department at Woods Hole Oceanographic Institution in Massachusetts. As a young student, she was a state spelling bee champion in Florida and once lost in the eighth grade when she misspelled "haddock" (a kind of fish). She now specializes in deep-sea exploration.

What appealed to you about this career?

—Miranda N., age 12

"I wanted to be a deep-sea biologist since I was six years old."

—DR. STACE BEAULIEU

Rick: I always wanted to be an ocean-ographer or a marine biologist. I have always been interested in the earth, how large it seems, and how the oceans were—and remain—largely undiscovered and unexplored.

Stace: I wanted to be a deep-sea biologist since I was six years old. We got *National Geographic* magazine at home. There was an issue about the discovery of hydrothermal vents, and they had really interesting animals that I had never seen before. I grew up in southern Florida. In addition to being interested in deep-sea animals because they were so freaky looking, I was very lucky because I did a lot of snorkeling. I had a friend whose dad had a small boat. He would take us out snorkeling around local reefs.

Stace Beaulieu

If I wanted to be an oceanographer, what school subjects are most important?

—John N., age 9

Rick: Study as much science as you can, and learn math. Numbers are a key to the environment. I also believe strongly in a liberal arts education, where people are encouraged to

Rick Keil

learn about many different things from science to art and politics.

Stace: Any scientist needs a good basis in math and a diversity of science courses. I use math when I have to accumulate biological data. I do statistics for those data. When I'm measuring flow and current, I'm using math to measure the record of flow.

What do you do in a typical day?

–Claire R., age 10

Rick: I have a research and teaching job at a university, which means that I spend roughly half my time teaching classes and half my time helping with the research that goes on in my group. I am part of a group of professors, students, and technicians who study the chemistry of the oceans. I don't just teach in classrooms; many of our classes take place on ships or on the beach. So, each day is a little different from the next one. Some days I will never make it to the lab because I am knee-deep in mud, collecting samples. Other days I am trapped behind a desk taking care of paperwork or writing scientific papers about our findings.

Stace: I'm a biological oceanographer so on shore I spend some time in the lab looking at samples. I spend some time at my office working with spreadsheets of data or writing a report on my data. And then I spend time with my students, teaching or mentoring.

At sea, that's a very different day. You work *long* hours. It can have moments with a lot of excitement where you're deploying an instrument into the sea. The instrument could be something that collects a water sample or a sediment sample from the seafloor or it could be something that measures temperature or salinity (salt content). There can also be moments that are not too exciting—you're sitting at a console waiting for your instrument to go down. When you get a sample on board, it's high energy again because you're taking care of the sample.

How much time do you spend in and on the ocean?

—Claire R., age 10

Rick: I am at sea about six or eight weeks a year, but some years I'll be at sea for more than 14 weeks. I typically use small boats that only sleep six scientists, and we only go out for a week at a time. However, for some of the bigger projects I collaborate with other scientists, and we use quite large boats (300 feet long, five stories high) that can carry as many as 30 scientists for as long as seven or eight weeks at a time.

Stace: Researching the deep sea is very, very expensive. So we go to sea about one month every couple of years. There's a lot of planning involved.

Are you studying a wide field of subjects or are you focusing on a certain one?

—Finnegan B., age 9

Rick: Both actually. Our lab group uses organic chemicals to try and understand how the ocean behaves, so in one sense we study a single thing: organic chemicals in the environment. There is actually more organic goop dissolved in ocean water than there is organic material in all the land animals piled together. We try to understand where the organic goop comes from, how microscopic organisms use it to grow, and whether some of it can be extracted and used to determine the history of the oceans and how it is changing today because of the activities of humans.

Our lab focuses on a few types of chemicals, but we use them to help answer many questions. What happens to the material dissolved in river water when it enters the ocean? Where does it go? Does it help plankton grow or inhibit them? Are the parts of the ocean that are *disaerobic* (have too little oxygen in them for fish to breath) getting larger? How are the natural disaerobic areas changing? Are humans creating new ones due to our polluting the oceans?

Stace: Almost all my study sites are more than two miles deep. To explore these areas, I use tools that include *submersibles*. On our last cruise, we used a submersible called *Alvin*. It's the most advanced deep-diving submersible in the United States. Two scientists and one pilot fit inside. *Alvin* makes my cruise expensive.

Do you only study a particular (geographic) part of the ocean and if so which part?

—Claire R., age 10

Rick: Right now we are focused in three areas, the coastal zone along the edge of Washington State and Vancouver Island, British Columbia, the disaerobic zone in the eastern tropical North Pacific (off the Pacific coast of Mexico), and the disaerobic zone of the Arabian Sea.

Stace: Almost all of my research is in the equatorial Pacific. My most recent trip was near Mexico and Costa Rica. We were studying the hydrothermal vents along the mid-ocean ridge. There was an undersea volcanic eruption that occurred in January 2006, and we went to this area nine months later to look at how the animal communities were developing there.

Do oceanographers work alone or in a group?

—Maren H., age 11

Rick: Most oceanographers work as members of a team. You have your own research and responsibilities, and you are part of a bigger team with bigger goals than what you can do all by yourself.

Stace: You're always collaborating with other scientists. Sometimes you work alone—you analyze samples or you write about your samples. But you're always getting feedback at all levels. When you write a paper you give it to your colleagues or students for comments. When you're sitting at a microscope looking at a sample, you do it alone, but you often share. Today, I was looking at some sediment that was collected at 4,000 meters depth (more than two miles) off the coast of California. I was scanning the sediment for small animals that live among the sediment grain. I shared what I was looking at with two students who were nearby.

Do oceanographers work in labs?

—*Maren H., age 11*

Rick: Yes, definitely! Our lab work is as much fun and as important as our field work. Many chemical oceanographers use lab facilities to measure compounds in the oceans at levels as low as parts-per-trillion, and then analyze samples to determine how minute concentrations of certain chemicals allow organisms to find each other or to find food (olfactory cues) or how chemicals influence reproduction, settling, growth, etc.

Stace: I spend part of my day sitting in a lab. Most people hate sitting at the microscope as long as I do. The lab I work in has several different kinds of microscopes—many tubes and vials. I mainly use regular light microscopes and every so often I use a scanning electron microscope. We look at the genes in sea creatures—the DNA.

Are there rules that you have to follow when being an oceanographer?

—*Maren H., age 11*

Rick: There are written rules for lab and ship safety. But I think the greatest rule that scientists try to follow is to be ethical in their research. Our ethical duty as oceanographers is to help determine how the oceans work, why they are the way they are, and to help determine the best ways to protect the oceans from harm.

Stace: There are so many rules! You need permission to go out to sea and cross into other nations' territorial waters. The submersible *Alvin* has tons and tons of rules. The engineering in getting humans safely down to the bottom of the sea involves many rules, including what kinds of clothes you wear inside the sub. Back at the lab, you follow rules as far as handling chemicals. When you're writing a paper and reporting your data, you really have to follow rules on how you do statistics by which you analyze your data.

What is your favorite thing to do in your job?

—Milo N., age 9

Rick: Discovery is exciting. Whether it is discovering a new feature of the oceans such as a ridge or hydrothermal vent or discovering something smaller about how a microorganism grows, one of the joys of being an oceanographer is discovering new things about the world.

Stace: In the lab, I really like taking photographs of things through the microscope [such as] small animals and even larvae. At sea, a favorite thing to do is to rig the mooring. You put together a mooring or an anchored structure of instruments that you deploy over the ship. It's also scary because if you mess up you lose your instrument.

What is the ocean like at night?

—Claire R., age 10

Rick: It was scary at first, but after a while I got used to it and it became fun. Most of the ocean is dark both day and night, so the ocean doesn't really change that much at night. It is like swimming through a dark forest with a flashlight.

Stace: The main reason to scuba dive at night is because you see different animals at night and many have *bioluminescence*. That means they have their own internal light that will light up in darkness. When I teach invertebrates we do some of the sampling at night because it's much easier to find the invertebrates then. That's when they come out. A good example is sea urchins and lobsters. At day, they're hiding from their predators. But at night you go scuba diving with dive lights around here and it's like ants because they're walking around all over the place.

What past invention or work of oceanographers do you most admire?

−John N., age 9

Rick: I am most impressed with people's ability to figure things out, so I admire the many people who figured out plate tectonics or deep water currents. Alfred Wegener, Harald Sverdrup, Roger Revelle, and others helped understand what are today the fundamentals of oceanography.

Stace: For an invention, I admire the multiple corer. It takes multiple cores of ocean floor sediment. You basically drop this instrument over the side of your ship. It's weighted and it goes down to the bottom of the ocean. You pull it up and you have these perfect sediment cores.

Some of the best work I admire was done in the 1970s when they discovered hydrothermal vents and it was the work by microbiologists that allowed us to understand that creatures there were supported by *chemosynthesis* as opposed to *photosynthesis*. Normally, all over our planet we see green plants and everything is supported by the sun through photosynthesis. But there at the bottom of the ocean, a mile or two deep, were thriving communities that are not supported by sunlight but by the chemicals coming out of the earth's interior. The transfer of the energy from the chemicals to the animals occurs through the bacteria, through the microbes.

CHAPTER 7

Virtual Apprentice

OCEANOGRAPHER FOR A DAY

Here's your chance to try an oceanographer's flippers on for size. You can tackle these activities on your own or make them into a school project where you share discoveries with your classmates. (Note that we've listed time according to the 24-hour maritime clock that oceanographers use aboard ship, so 13:00 would be the same as 1:00.)

8:00 Start the day with some aquatic exploration. Set a goal of observing five different types of marine life. If you are lucky enough to live near water—salty or fresh—see if you can arrange a field trip with a teacher or parent. Bring paper and pencil with you to record your findings. And carry a baggie or jar to hold any specimens you discover (seashells, for example). If not, see what you can find at the local pet store or go online for some Internet surfing.

9:00 Time for a little lab work. Make a saltwater solution: Fill a glass with water and stir in 1 teaspoon of table salt—about the same salinity as seawater. Compare your homemade salt water with a glass of fresh water. Taste and smell both, then crack a whole raw egg into each glass and watch what happens. Record your findings.

10:00 Computers have had a big impact on ocean science. Join an online expedition or visit a site where you can follow a live Web cam on a marine critter such as a jellyfish or an otter. Here's a place in cyberspace to embark from: http://www.h2o.com/channels/cams.htm. Create a timeline that describes what a jellyfish or otter does all day.

11:00 Create a mini oil spill. Spread out newspaper to catch drips and fill a baking pan with sand, rocks, and salted water to create a mini ocean environment. Assemble some Q-tips, paper towels, string, cotton balls, cornstarch, dishwashing detergent, and anything else you think might help clean up oil. First, record your predictions about what will happen when you add oil to the environment. Then slowly pour a teaspoonful of oil (a dark-colored oil like olive or sesame oil is best) into the middle of the pan. Watch where the oil spill goes as you agitate the pan and blow on the water to simulate the motion of the waves. Try to contain and clean up the spill with your supplies. What works and what doesn't? What happens as time passes? Try cleaning oil off sand and rocks—which is easier? Compare what actually happens with your predictions.

12:00 What's for lunch? Sushi, tuna salad, or fish sticks, of course! The Omega-3 oils in fish make it great for your brain.

13:00 Cook up your own deep-sea vent. Fill a large glass container with ice water. Take a smaller glass bottle and tie a string around its neck. Fill the small bottle with very hot water (ask your teacher or a parent to help you) and a few drops of food coloring. Keep the bottle upright and carefully lower it to the bottom of the big glass container. Make a chart with two columns. In the first column, write a prediction of what you expect will happen. In the second column, write a description of what actually does happen.

14:00 Make some waves! Fill a plastic water bottle halfway with water and four drops of food coloring. Use a small funnel and add enough vegetable oil to fill the rest of the bottle. Cover the threads where the cap goes on with a little glue and screw it on tight. Now tilt and rock the bottle back and forth to create motions like the waves.

15:00 Put all your findings together in a research notebook.

16:00 Investigate three things you can do at home or at your school to protect the world's oceans. Think about this and get creative. Make a poster that you could use to encourage other people to follow your example.

17:00 Finally, reward yourself and wind up your day the way many real oceanographers do: Watch an episode of *SpongeBob SquarePants*, the cartoon that was actually created by an oceanographer.

Virtual Apprentice

OCEANOGRAPHER: FIELD REPORT

If this is your book, use the space below to jot down a few notes about the Virtual Apprentice experience (or use a blank sheet of paper if the book doesn't belong to you). What did you do? What did you learn? Which activity did you enjoy the most? Which was the most challenging?

8:00 AQUATIC EXPLORATION: _____

_____

_____

_____

9:00 LAB WORK: _____

_____

_____

_____

10:00 ONLINE EXPEDITION: _____

_____

_____

_____

11:00 OIL SPILL CLEAN-UP: _____

_____

_____

_____

12:00 LUNCH: _____
_____
_____

13:00 DEEP-SEA VENT: _____
_____
_____
_____

14:00 MAKING WAVES: _____
_____
_____
_____

15:00 MARITIME DATA: _____
_____
_____
_____

16:00 GET WET!: _____
_____
_____
_____

17:00 CHILL OUT: _____
_____
_____
_____

Count Me In (or Out)

ARE YOU READY TO TAKE THE PLUNGE?

Do you think oceanography is the perfect field for you, or have you got cold (wet) feet about the whole idea of working in such a scientific profession? If you're still adrift, the following questions and writing prompts may help set you on course. Record your answers and responses on a separate sheet of paper or in your ship's log and review them before you launch your career in the ocean sciences.

Three aspects of oceanography I'd like to learn more about include:

1. _____

2. _____

3. _____

I could take the following steps to increase my knowledge of the oceans:

_____

_____

_____

_____

Imagine that you're channel surfing and you come across a TV special about the search for *Architeuthis dux,* the giant squid. Which of the following best expresses your reaction?:

❑ I keep on flipping. Who cares about an oversized calamari when *Mr. Meaty* is on?

❑ I watch it for a couple minutes until the science stuff starts to bore me. Why don't they show a death battle between a sperm whale and a giant squid? That would be awesome!

❑ I'm glued to the set, waiting to see actual pictures of this amazing creature that has managed to elude humans for so long. I wouldn't miss this for the world!

❑   Underwater footage always gives me the creeps—it's murky and weird down there! I change the channel until I find a cute little program about the Mongolian death worm.

❑   Why waste time channel surfing? I grab my board and head over to the beach for some real surfing while the waves are high.

(If you chose number 3, you definitely have a real interest in the ocean and the mysteries that it holds. If you picked number 5, your love for the wild waves could mean that oceanography is a natural career choice for you.)

Here are three things I can do to help conserve the world's oceans:

1. _____

2. _____

3. _____

I think the next big marine discovery will be:

_____

_____

_____

_____

_____

_____

I want to:

❑   Read all about it from the comfort of my cozy chair.

❑   Be part of the team that makes that incredible discovery.

❑   Be the multibillionaire who puts up the money for that discovery.

❑   See the headline on the front page of the newspaper before I flip past to the women's basketball scores.

❑   Create a work of art based on this new information and how it changes what it means to be human.

APPENDIX

More Resources for Young Oceanographers

BOOKS

Bonner, Nigel. *Seals and Sea Lions of the World*. New York: Facts on File, 2004.

Bonner, Nigel. *Whales of the World*. New York: Facts on File, 2003.

Dipper, Frances. *DK Guide to the Oceans*. New York: Dorling Kindersley, 2004.

Gerdes, Louise I. *Endangered Oceans*. San Diego, Calif.: Greenhaven Press, 2003.

Green, Jen. *The Oceans and Seas: Atlantic Ocean*. Milwaukee, Wisc.: Gareth Stevens, 2006.

Green, Jen. *The Oceans and Seas: Pacific Ocean*. Milwaukee, Wisc.: Gareth Stevens, 2006.

Lindop, Laurie. *Science on the Edge: Venturing the Deep Sea*. Minneapolis: Twenty-First Century Books, 2005.

Littlefield, Cindy A. *Awesome Ocean Science: Investigating the Secrets of the Underwater World*. Nashville, Tenn.: Ideals Publications, 2002.

Pedersen, Traci Steckel. *Reading Essentials in Science: Oceanography*. Logan, Iowa: Perfection Learning, 2007.

Prevost, John F. *The Oceans and Seas: Arctic Ocean*. Milwaukee, Wisc.: Gareth Stevens, 2003.

Prevost, John F. *The Oceans and Seas: Indian Ocean*. Milwaukee, Wisc.: Gareth Stevens, 2003.

Rhodes, Mary Jo. *Undersea Encounters: Life on a Coral Reef*. Danbury, Conn.: Children's Press, 2007.

Rhodes, Mary Jo. *Undersea Encounters: Octopuses and Squids*. Danbury, Conn.: Children's Press, 2006.

Schlank, Carol Hilgartner. *A Clean Sea: The Rachel Carson Story*. Marina del Rey, Calif.: Cascade Pass, 2002.

Steel, Rodney. *Sharks of the World*. New York: Facts on File, 2003.

PROFESSIONAL ASSOCIATIONS

Cousteau Society
710 Settlers Landing Road, Hampton, Virginia 23669
http://www.cousteau.org

National Oceanic and Atmospheric Administration (NOAA)
http://www.noaa.gov

Oceanography Society
P.O. Box 1931, Rockville, Maryland 20849-1931
http://www.tos.org

WEB SITES

Monterey Bay Aquarium
http://www.mbayaq.org

Women in Oceanography
http://www.womenoceanographers.org

Woods Hole Oceanographic Institution
http://www.divediscover.whoi.edu

INDEX